FOREVER OR NEVER

KENNETH POLACK

ISBN 979-8-88945-418-2 (softcover)
ISBN 979-8-88945-419-9 (ebook)

This book is a work of fiction. Names, characters, places, and incidents are the
product of the author's imagination or are used fictitiously. Any resemblance
to actual locales, events, or persons, living or dead, is purely coincidental.

Printed in the United States of America.

Brilliant Books Literary
137 Forest Park Lane Thomasville
North Carolina 27360 USA

This is a story where fantasy and reality blend, where shedding light can cast shadows of unknowns, the hidden truth of parts each of us will play! Forever-sought questions, answered! Mysteries revealed! Made known in your mind: death's true purpose!

CHAPTER 1

Forever or Never

I'm sure each of us, at some point in our lives, feel we have a decent grasp on things, you know, life and the reality of it. Starting your day knowing all that has been taught to you is true (reality) solidly anchored in your life. But how many of us are forced to completely rethink our understanding of what we thought we knew?

I'm Ted. This is my story.

It all started when I was twenty-three in small town in California. Myself along with others noticed strange lights in the sky every couple of days or so.

This went on for what seemed like a month. I was amazed at what I was seeing: objects in the sky that could only be things flying. But so fast! Impossible direction changes. Single objects becoming many; many objects becoming one. I'm pretty sure everyone in our town had a chance to see something odd in the sky.

I remember watching spectacles in the sky and asking people around me, "Are you seeing this? Did you see that?" They always answered yes. The odd thing was we weren't always seeing the same thing. But the obvious question we all had was "What is it?"

One time shortly before dark, I saw a city perched on the clouds. And there were things moving about the city, shadows, something! Once I heard a loud noise like a train screeching to a halt. But the deafening sound seemed to come from the sky, and when I looked up, I saw the clouds turn a reddish orange and part as if a massive invisible object push them aside!

And another time I was completely dumbfounded when I saw what looked like a couple of fingertips and thumb touching the sky as if our world was tiny and they were giant. Their fingers seeming to touch our sky and brush something away and then it was gone!

Some of the things I saw were only there for a split second and impossible to describe. I wondered if I was imagining things! Once I watched as a ship or saucer traveling in a straight line disappear and reappear several times as if it was phasing in and out of invisibility.

Lights are one thing, but the things I saw forced me to reexamine the reality I thought I knew. The entire town saw things. Were we all delusional?

CHAPTER 2

You know, I used to think people easily dismissing unexplained phenomena in the sky was strange because I know we all saw fascinating things. I mean, how do you just unsee something? But that's nothing. Most people denying what's right in front of their eyes is just the tip of the iceberg.

We've all heard stories throughout our lives that made us wonder. That's it! Where's the rest? What else happened? Who else knows about this? Why haven't I heard of this before?

The kind of stories that makes you think to yourself, *This can't be true. This must be fake and made up.* Just because of the way it was presented to you—secondhand, so to speak.

No authority figure making it known, just someone saying, "Hey did you hear about?" or "Did you know?" or how about, "I heard once a long time ago." It's so easy to dismiss something credible when it's shrouded in obscurities.

I'll give you an example. If you heard about a fantastically bizarre and mysterious story that happened in some unknown part of the world, and this story is told to you by a coworker, and if you were to ask them where they heard this story, and he or she said they heard it from there uncle who heard it from his neighbor that heard it from there mailman's brother, you probably wouldn't give it the same attention. You would if you heard it on the ten o'clock news. It just seems to me that things only matter when they're made to matter, or when it's made to matter to you!

So there I was living in this small town, and like many others, I've been seeing lights in the sky on and off for about three weeks. And I felt I didn't have the same opinion that everybody else did. Authority figures had said we had nothing to worry about. So why worry? That was the general consensus.

I guess you could say I was concerned about the lights, and I was also concerned that no one seemed to care.

Anyone that had seen the lights knew what we were seeing didn't match what they were telling us it was.

But most people didn't seem to mind because someone that they felt knew more than they did said they had nothing to worry about.

So explained away it went! People of authority, quoted by our town paper, told the town folk we had all seen recently launched weather balloons. And other phenomenon was attributed to swamp gas and strange atmospheric anomalies.

Such is life! They were all too eager to get back to theirs. On with the daily grind day after day. People pretty much felt the lights weren't worth worrying about.

To them, ignoring it made more sense than wondering about something unexplainable. I guess I would have fell into the same mindset had it not been for the continuous strange occurrences that forever changed my life!

CHAPTER 3

One day, a few days since the commotion with the lights, I was heading back to my car from the corner store when I saw old man Edward. He was coming out of the alley, just near where I parked. Edward was an older man somewhere in his sixties I think, anyhow, he seemed a bit odd to me, and I remember being told I should avoid him, but today, he was heading right toward me.

He seemed to be in a panic, and both of his hands were cupped on his face. And I could see red, bright red, you know, the color of bloodred! The closer I got to my car, the closer he got to me. By the time, I was thinking, *I don't need this today, whatever this is.* We were only a few feet away from one another.

He was wailing and moving his head all about! My hands were shaking so bad, I couldn't get my key into the car door. I couldn't tell if he was trying to keep his head from moving by holding it with his hands, or if it was the other way around. But I could clearly see that the red was indeed blood! And Edward was having a bad day!

I looked around in a panic to see if anybody was seeing what I was seeing and could maybe intervene. I just wanted to not be there! Just then, he fell to his knees, crying, and carrying on, his hands still cupped tightly to his face, blood everywhere!

At this point, it was me, just me! Like it or not, I was right in the middle of this situation. I saw no one else that could help. I told myself, *Man up! And try not to get any blood on you.*

As I got closer, the severity of his dilemma came into view. It looked as if he was trying to tear his face off! I couldn't believe what I was seeing. He was yelling and screaming at the top of his lungs. I thought for a second that maybe he had gone mad! I hollered out, "What's wrong?"

He was tugging, tearing, and ripping! As he thrashed about, I could see pieces of flesh dangling from his face and hanging from his fingers. He was actually tearing one of his hands from his face! Blood was everywhere! He ripped half his face off when his hand finally came free.

There was one finger left, the pinky. It was somehow hanging on his face. I couldn't understand. This was all happening so fast right in front of me! It was the last finger to go. I watched as his frantic tearing motion snapped his pinky into and left it dangling from his right eyebrow. There it was, two knuckles of a pinky just dangling from his face!

I tried to calm him down. He was confused, and I know I was! I asked him what happened. I asked if he knew why his hands were stuck to his face. He said it was punishment!

He stated, "This is how they left me. They said it's punishment for keeping something that wasn't mine to keep!" And that his mind was invaded. He didn't seem sure of the place and time. He asked me what year it was and asked, "Am I here?"

I was thinking, *Wow, what would cause a man to go off the deep end like this? And who would do this to someone?*

For a moment but only for a moment, I thought maybe some kids played a joke on him. You see, I took Edward for a homeless drunk! So I thought maybe while he was passed out in the alley from a drunken stupor, perhaps kids had superglued his fingers and hands to his face.

I tried lifting the other hand free from his face, just to see how stuck it was. And boy was he stuck! It felt like his hand was stuck to his skull! I told him it would be all right. I told him I would get him to the hospital and that he wasn't going to die. You know the things you would probably tell somebody in a situation like this.

But it was more than that. I felt totally sympathetic to his dilemma. I was no longer fearful of this man. I just wanted to help!

Soon there was no longer a need to try to calm Edward down. He was becoming calmer with each passing minute. I left him for a moment and went to the corner payphone and called the local sheriff who happened to be a buddy of mine. I asked him to come down and help.

When I got back to Edward, he was sitting up, one hand still stuck to his face. I sat down next to him on the sidewalk. He looked at me, one of his eyes peering through his fingers and the other half blocked by a dangling broken, bloody pinky!

He asked me, "Would you want to know things that most never will? If given the chance to know your own destiny." He talked about things like how little we know of our own existence! He said, "What would you sacrifice to know your true purpose?"

His direct and comprehensive questioning made me feel as if he had a clear grasp of his current situation! The way he talked, it sent chills down my spine! The things he said and the way he said them. I found myself transfixed!

So what was supposed to be a quick trip to the store for me turned out to be the first of many strange and remarkable experiences to come because I told Edward, "Yes! I want to know!"

CHAPTER 4

The payphone I just came from started ringing. It was the sheriff. He was basically asking, "What?" He needed me to repeat what I just told him. I guess even though I thought I was clear on the phone, I obviously wasn't. I explained to him again the situation and asked him to send an ambulance as well. He still didn't know what the hell I was talking about, but he did what I asked and came right away.

When the sheriff and ambulance arrived, Edward clammed up. He answered very few questions the sheriff had for him and said he didn't know anything about what happened to him. The sheriff pulled me off to the side to ask me what I knew.

I told him everything I knew. After that, the sheriff summarized his own theory about what he figured had happened. The sheriff said, "I'll bet you some kids found him passed out drunk in the back alley and pranked him and superglued his hands to his face."

I got a chuckle deep down inside for just a second thinking the sheriff thought exactly the same thing I thought. But now, now I was pretty sure there was more to it, but I didn't let on. I just looked at the sheriff and said, "Maybe!"

* * *

At the hospital.

The doctor said that his hands weren't superglued to his face after all. He said they were actually healed that way after being skinned open. I couldn't believe what I was hearing. He said it looked like the wounds had been healed for years!

In other words, somebody had cut open his fingers and face and then let them heal after putting the wounds together. The doctor said it was even more than that. It was as if the bones of his fingers were fused to his skull! Hearing that gave me those chills down my spine again!

The doctor went on explaining how he admired the attention to the precision and accuracy of the incisions and the lack of scar tissue. Edward was sedated, and off to the operating room they went. He was operated on for hours.

The sheriff told me they did a good job operating on him. The doctor told him that this was the most bizarre thing he ever encountered, and he'd been practicing medicine for thirty-five years. He said removing his hand was like making incisions for the first time.

The sheriff and I got together at least three times after this, you know, to try to get some resolve. Have it explained to us, or at least explain it to ourselves in a way that would satisfy the constant curiosity and wondering of what happened.

Where's Edward? He disappeared days later. And why didn't anyone else care about this? The third time the sheriff and I met, he told me that his inquiries yielded no answers. He said all inquiries just sort of petered out and that he was actually told by his superiors to let it go and get on with other things. That was the last time we met to discuss the matter.

Now something like this you think would turn up in the news, right? Well, I thought so too. But to this day, it never has! Just like the lights, it seems nobody cares!

About three months later, after I thought I learned how to let go, the obsession of wondering what I witnessed began to consume my thoughts again. I was having crazy, crazy dreams unlike anything I've ever had before.

Dreaming and feeling purposely, powerfully, destination-desiring, unwavering, abundant potential beaming toward familiar homesick thoughts of belonging! Incredible tickle in my stomach! I awakened from what can only be described as flying in yet another indescribable dream!

Making me to start my day wondering why. Why are we here? Who are we? Where did we come from? What does it all mean? Who am I?

I found myself more and more thinking back to the lights. I've come to believe that it wasn't us, us as in all of us humans. I believed it was otherworldly. I had no proof. I only knew how I felt! Also, what was up with that old man Edward? Unrealistically uncanny, just than a knock at the door.

CHAPTER 5

Upon opening the door, my pulse quickened. I was just thinking about him! For there stood old man Edward. He didn't look like the down-on-his-luck bum I remember. He looked like a man, just a normal guy.

Normal except for his face. I knew it was Edward because of the face! The damage to the right side of his face was extensive. There were several smaller scars along with three deep and long purple scars! The left side of his face was less disfigured thanks to the surgeon's work but still pretty bad!

Stunned and hoping not to be recognized, I said, "Yes? Can I help you?" Half hoping he was there for a reason other than what deep down I knew he was really here for!

I was waiting for a pause at the doorway that would be silent and awkward. But without skipping a beat, Edward said, "Do you still want answers, Ted?" I told him I don't know. I'm not sure if I care to know. I almost wanted the past to be forgotten.

I told him I wasn't sure if I should be involved. He told me I was already involved. He said my involvement started before we met and before the lights!

I didn't expect him to say that. I felt dazed and confused. I felt that transfixed feeling like the first time we met. A part of me just wanted to close the door. But I couldn't because he was right!

"I don't know what you're talking about."

He said, "Your dreams, the ones you have had since the lights. Do you really think they're normal?" He said, "I feel you should know what I know. If what I say now doesn't intrigue you enough to continue, I will walk away and take what I know with me!"

Reluctantly, I invited him in for coffee! We sat at the kitchen table and started to talk.

"So what happened that day on the street? How and why did your hands get stuck to your face?" I asked him.

Edward replied, "It's like I said. It was a form of punishment."

"Punishment by who?" I asked. "What for?" I asked.

"There's much you need to know!" As he tilted his coffee cup to take a sip, I noticed a deformed pinky and a scar going clear around the second knuckle, furthering my belief that this was indeed Edward. "But for now, do you remember your dreams?"

"Not all of them," I said.

"Are they strange?" asked Edward, charged with emotion.

"Actually, yes, they are," I told him.

"Think back to your first dreams after the lights and the ones you've been having sense."

I knew which dreams he meant. He was talking about the dreams that were scaring the shit out of me! And I knew this had something to do with the lights!

I said, "I'm not sure if I remember."

He said, "bullshit!" He said, "If you want to know the truth, be truthful with me." He knew I was lying. It's like he could see right through me. Somehow, this person I barely knew, he's in my head!

And somehow, I know he's honest and truthful. He told me it was important that I should know all he knows.

These dreams I've had since the lights were not normal. Edward was absolutely right about that. They were the most vivid and emotional dreams I had ever had in my life.

The first strange dream I can remember after the lights was before that day I ever met Edward. I told him I remember being in a strange room, and someone was there with me. Someone in the same situation, helpless like me.

I was not able to see the other person, but still, I knew they were there and that they were going through what I was going through. "And there was something else," Edward interjected, "questions without words. Yes! A voice in your head that was not yours. Yes!"

"Yes!" I said.

"Questions put forth not with words but of images provoking feelings and emotions!"

Again, I said, "Yes!"

I asked Edward how he could know this. He said, "Because it was me. I was there with you!"

I said, "Were you in my dream?"

Edward said, "You could say you were in mine!"

"Okay, you're freaking me out a little bit," I told him.

He said, "How many times did they kill you?"

"What? Killed?" I said. As soon as I thought about what he just said, memories from nowhere smacked me right between the eyes. I had goose bumps. I started breaking out in a sweat.

He said, "What do you remember?"

I told him, "Once, I remember being returned to my bed. Something was gently placing me in my bed, floating to my pillow like a feather ever so softly. But I felt it was wrong, misleading. What seemed to be an act of kindness was to be shattered in an instant like every bone in my body! I almost couldn't breathe remembering this!"

CHAPTER 6

I remembered a force that felt like the weight of the world surrounded my body and ever so slowly crushed me to bits! I remember I couldn't scream, I couldn't breathe, and I was dead! I could remember this clearly with every detail as if it had actually happened. But I was alive!

Without pause, that memory instantly triggered another. I could remember both arms and both legs penned down unable to move, all my limbs being pulled tightly in opposite directions, pulling harder and harder until I was separated!

Images of torture continued over and over until I approached exhaustion, then the image of jagged icicle shaped fingers approached me. I could feel a cold sharpness pressing, pushing, and penetrating my chest as if to scoop out my insides!

Remembering this was excruciating! The intense pain of those cold sharp fingers penetrating my chest, I could feel it searching until it found its grip! I felt my life weakening as it tugged.

I found myself tugging back as if we both had a grip on whatever this thing was after. I remember the urgency of keeping hold and not letting go! And then darkness! I had to sit down. I felt sick! So many emotions all at once!

"There's others. There's others that aren't us," I said. I started remembering segments of disturbing encounters in my past. "They are here now. And they are doing this to us! They are not like us! They did this to me? Why?" I could remember bits, pieces, fragments, slowly more and more details!

Edward said, "That's the tool they use. They use dreams against us. This is how they find what they're looking for."

"Who are they?" I asked. "They're aliens, aren't they?" I exclaimed.

Edward exclaimed back, "Of course, they are!"

I wouldn't say I was totally caught off guard with this information. Deep down, I knew it already, but now, wow. Wow! This really is real! I felt buzzy and light-headed. I needed to wrap my head around this.

"So you say they're using my dreams against me?"

Edward said, "No, not your dreams, memories of other people's realities, events that really happened to other people." Edward could tell by the look on my face that I didn't understand.

Edward went on to explain that in the past, and still even now, atrocities are performed on humans, deaths especially. Millions of recorded events each with their own emotional value (dreams, if you will).

With these countless emotionally charged dreams, up to and including death, they can be placed in our minds to elicit a reaction and then effectively erase the memory of it when they're done.

"What are they looking for?" I asked.

"There's more," he said. He explained that phrases could trigger my memory, like the question "How many times did they kill you?" Edward went on to explain that it was a combination, part dream and part memory. And that I may soon start to remember more. Death dreams, he called them.

Edward asked if I would give him time to help me understand. I told Edward he needed to explain what's going on. "What is this all about?" I demanded. "Tell me!"

CHAPTER 7

Edward wanted to show me something. He asked if I would go on a short trip with him in the morning. He said it would help me understand to see with my own eyes as he explains. I had to know! I agreed, and we set out early.

During the trip, we didn't talk much. It was awkward. Edward turned the radio on and kept it loud. When Edward did talk, he told me it was absolutely about the lights. He said everything we do daily is directly connected!

I asked Edward, "What do they want from me?"

Edward said, "The same thing they want from every person on this planet!" Edward went on telling me that anyone thinking of aliens coming to our planet and what they would want all got it wrong!

"Ideas such as they would enslave us, or wiping us out to take our planet, or they want our planets resources, or that we are a zoo planet, or that they just want to eat us—all wrong.

They just want something that is inside us. That's all! And to understand that entails you to understand who and what people are!"

After about an hour or so, we arrived in the desert, the middle of nowhere. After running out of dirt road, Edward grabbed a backpack, and we walked for a bit until we came across an opening that looked like a cave or mine or something.

Edward handed me a flashlight and a rolled-up hazmat suit. I said, "What's the suit for? Is it dangerous?"

Edward chuckled, "Ha, ha. Define dangerous? Some would say being alive is dangerous!"

Edward assured me it was just to keep us clean. That sounded okay with me. We turned on the flashlights, and in we went. On the drive over, Edward did tell me that a buddy of his showed him this place years ago. We must've made our way several hundred feet down this dirty cavern until we came across a pool of water.

This is where Edward told me that when his friend reached the water table, he came back with scuba gear to explore farther. He was just hoping to find some artifacts, maybe an old pic or shovel or even a mining cart, something of value!

Edward's friend splashed into the water, and he found he was not in water but in another place. Edward said, "That's where we're going." He could see I was skeptical, so he went first. As he slipped into the water, my skepticism remained. It just looked like he went into some water. But I had to follow.

As I stepped into the water and lowered myself in. It felt wet on my suits. As I got waist-deep, I felt a tug on my leg, and in I went. The next thing I know, Edward is pulling me into a shiny, clean, dry cave!

I'm dry as a bone and covered in dirt. Edward said, "This is where we should leave the suits so we can move around and not leave tracks."

I said, "Tracks! Should we be here? Is someone here?"

Edward said, "There shouldn't be anyone here, but let's play it safe. We'll keep it clean and whisper."

"What is this place?" I whispered.

"For now, passageways," Edward whispered back.

Trying to explain when you know things aren't as they seem. It's difficult! Slipping through a camouflaged shroud of what looked and felt like water and then arriving in an environment that is completely different from the one you just left. Let's just say it takes a second to regain yourself!

From dirty rock to passageways of polished smooth well-lit, ovalish-shaped corridors that felt like glass, there was a slight breeze with the perfect temperature air that smelled refreshing. I was excited and intrigued!

I could see only one direction to go but for only a short distance. What appeared to be the end of the tunnel as we approached now looked blurry and like moving smoke, wisping farther away as you approached, making more corridor to follow.

We walked for what seemed like a half mile. Edward stopping a few times along the way making sure we were on course.

"So these tunnels are made by aliens?" I asked Edward.

"Absolutely!" Edward replied. "Well! To be more specific, the technology is theirs, but the tunnels here now are ours, for now anyway. It's confusing!" said Edward.

I said, "How do you know where you're going?"

"You can choose your direction with your mind," Edward explained. "These tunnels are thought directed. We just need to continue going left and up."

CHAPTER 8

Ahead appears blurry. You can almost see the smoke carving the corridor as it wisps its way through. It's confusing to the eye. The corridor is perfectly lit, a sort-of incandescent. You can feel movement while walking through the passageways, a sort of sensation of speed!

As we get closer to a blurry spot, we see intersections giving us options. They go under, or up and over. Seems to be whatever your mind chooses. Edward said, "It's simple. The direction you need to go is the direction chosen!"

We make our way through a few more blurry inter-sections, we round a corner and approach what appear to be three smoky black oval mirrors. "The middle one is ours," Edward said. We step up to our reflection and walk through.

On the other side, we step out between two giant rocks to find ourselves in a forest. "What?" I said. "Where are we? How did we get to a forest?"

Edward explained, "Even though we only walked about a half mile, we traveled a great distance. It's complicated." The tunnels move through the earth, and they are there and not there.

"And why did we come here?" I said.

"We're meeting someone."

"Who?" I asked.

"A friend," said Edward. Just then, I felt a buzzing and heard a faint ringing in my ears. The hairs on my arms started to lift. And a gray being stepped out of a boulder! And he started speaking to us. At least I think it was speaking.

I found myself frozen. I couldn't move. I couldn't speak. I wasn't even sure if I was breathing. All I could do was stare at this creature that was somehow speaking to me.

My gaze, which became obsessed, studied the creature. It was standing maybe four-and-a-half feet tall. It had a skinny neck and a thin jaw. It had a small mouth and almost no nose. Its large eyes were the color of gun metal. Its gaze upon me felt as if it was peeling layers, and I knew it understood me at my deepest self. It's enormous head obviously boasting vast intelligence!

Through its subtle gestures and movements, I could see tendons and muscles move just under the skin of its neck as veins with whatever blood this being was filled with pulsated. It articulated its meaning to me.

Its strange clothing looked as the creature did. It was hard to tell what was clothing and what was skin. Some parts of the creature that I could tell was skin appeared dry and chalky, but the wrinkles and crevices looked moist and silvery.

The craziest thing were the eyes. They were mesmerizing! It had a light hint of a brow with a scowl above its left eye. It didn't look real! This thing looked fragile but scary as hell!

When the alien got done communicating, it just turned around and walked back into the boulder and was gone. The buzzing had stopped, so did the ringing in my ears. A second or two later, I was able to move again. I walked over and smacked the rock the creature had gone into, and yeah, it was a rock!

"Is it no wonder our ancestors thought it was magic?"

Edward went on saying, "This was nothing, just the tip of the iceberg. Their abilities are mind-blowing! That's why I think it's best I show you things as I explain."

"So who was that gray creature?" I asked.

"He's an ally. He helped me before."

"He's an alien?" I asked.

Edward said, "Yes! He doesn't believe as the others, and very few of them believe as he does. But they made it their mission to help those they can. He's called Hermes!" Edward went on to explain that he has received help from him in the past.

Strangely, in those brief moments while the alien spoke, I understood more about why I was there. It was to obtain some technology the alien was giving us an advantage but handing it to us was not allowed. It made clear that there were rules! But the alien did let us know where we could find it. And somehow, I knew how important it was to find this technology.

CHAPTER 9

"I know where to go to get the device!" I exclaimed.

"So do I!" Edward exclaimed back.

We went back down into the corridors and made a couple rights at the intersections and emerged into a large multiroom space. The main chamber was as big as a concert hall. And within it were many smaller rooms that we would have to search.

I thought for sure we would be discovered. Edward assured me we had enough time to get in and get out if we split up. We needed to find the device! "What are we looking for? What does it look like?" I asked Edward. Just then, a flashback of when the alien was communicating. "I could see the device!"

I don't remember the creature describing the device when we were in the forest. I just remember him stressing the urgency to find it! But now, I clearly remember him communicating the full description of the device. So weird!

I told Edward, "Never mind. I know what we're looking for. It's a small four-inch cylinder with a loop that goes around your fingers and fits in the palm of your hand. And it's black and silver and smooth like polished rock!"

Edward said, "Yep!"

I said, "I'm not sure how I know, but I know!"

"And for now, that's all you need to know!" said Edward. "Now, let's split up and go find it and remember, be quiet!" Edward exclaimed.

As I entered one of the rooms and started looking for the device, I could see a kind of shelving or cubbyholes along the walls. I quickly looked through several rooms, and in these shelves were many strange devices.

There were different-sized balls in many colors. I saw devices shaped like pinecones. There were things of metal. There were things of fabric. There were things on shelves in motion! There were devices of light, so many things I was tempted to touch. But once again out of nowhere, I remember it being conveyed by the creature, "Do not touch!" So I didn't! I was looking for one device in particular! The searching continued for what seemed like too long.

An object on a lower shelf caught my attention. A dark flat circle was floating several inches above the shelf, about the size of a Frisbee, and it was as thin as a razor with just enough contrast in the thick deep black to clearly see it was slowly swirling clockwise. As I knelt down to get a closer look, I could see there was depth to the darkness!

As I gazed into its depths, I was overwhelmed with thoughts of what we were doing. I remember wondering if we're ever going to get out of here. Suddenly, I was sitting in the passenger seat of Edward's car. We're driving, and he was explaining to me things he knew.

Just then, I felt a presence near me when I turned to look I was back in the room, and Edward was walking toward me. "I haven't found it, and we need to go!" Edward exclaimed. As I went to stand up, sitting on the shelf next to the swirling black mass was the device. There it was!

"Here it is!" I exclaimed.

As I grabbed the device, Edward said, "Good. We got to go. Move fast but be quiet!"

CHAPTER 10

As we returned to the corridors and started making our way back, I told Edward what I had experienced with the swirling black disk. "You say you found yourself in the car on our way back home?" Edward asked.

"Yeah," I said.

"You glimpsed the future!" said Edward. "The mass was spinning clockwise, so your conscious was transported forward in time. What were you thinking just before you found yourself in the car?" asked Edward.

"I was wondering if we were going to get out of there."

"Well, there you go. I didn't know until you start talking about it, but I remember being told about this device," said Edward.

"Let me guess. It just came to you?" I said. Edward chuckled, "Yeah!"

Edward went on saying that the device is one of two parts. "The one you experienced lets you see. When added to the second device, it allows you to go."

"Go? You mean actually go to the place you're seeing?" I asked.

"Uh, yes," Edward replied. "And if you have a disk rotating counterclockwise, it'll take you backward!"

I could tell Edward was remembering this information right then and there. He was explaining it to me as he was learning about it himself.

"You mean time travel?" I asked.

"Yeah," Edward replied. "So weird!" Edward mumbled. "Let me see the device you grabbed," Edward asked. "I know what it does."

As I handed him the device, I got a good look at Edward's fingers, and it reminded me of the day we met. His fingertips were pointy and thin as there was no meat between the skin and bone. His fingernails were oddly misshaped and sharp.

"I'll show you what this does. Stand in front of me." As I stood in front of Edward and watched, he placed the device on his fingers, moved his hand toward his chest, and he was gone!

I stood there for a moment whispering Edward's name. I walked all around where he had been. There was nothing. He was gone! A moment later, Edward reappeared across the corridor.

"We'll call this a mirror shield," Edward said as he pulled the device from his fingers.

"Wow!" I said. "Where did you go? You disappeared!"

"I could see and hear you!" Edward exclaimed.

"Awesome!" I said.

"Let's keep moving," said Edward.

As Edward and I made our way back toward our original entrance. Edward felt compelled to take a detour. He asked me if I was game. He said it was something I needed to see. I asked him, "How far?"

He said, "It's a little ways, maybe three quarters of a mile."

"By my calculations of traveling through these tunnels, that could put us thousands of miles from here."

Edward said, "Yes. I've been there. I think it's near the south pole." I was intrigued and totally energized from the things I had been experiencing!

"Wow! Okay, let's go," I said.

CHAPTER 11

As we set off back through the labyrinth of corridors, we encountered a downward slope, which turned into a stairway going down. Not like normal stairs though. The steps were shallow. I definitely felt the sensation of going down, the sensation of going downward was much greater than the shallowness of the steps!

The walk seemed easy and effortless, and I could feel that sensation of movement again. It wasn't long before we found ourselves at this place Edward wanted to take me.

Upon stepping out of a mirror at the end of the corridor, I could see blue sky below me and the earth above. As we completed stepping through the mirror, my view spun on its axis and was back to normal with blue skies above and earth below. I was dumbfounded once again as I stood on what appeared to be an observation platform on a cliff overlooking a deep crater!

"It doesn't make sense. We had been going downhill the whole time! How could we be on top of a mountain?"

Edward said, "I know. It's crazy! This is actually a volcano."

As I looked over the edge, I could see no bottom to the enormous cavern, just a faint light way down deep. Edward said, "This way." We walked over to another entrance near the platform. As we entered a hallway we were presented with dozens of small rooms.

As we stepped into the closest room, a mirrorlike door shut behind us. Edward asked me to stand next to him as he put the device on his fingers and raised his hand to his chest activating the mirror shield device.

I couldn't tell if it was working. It didn't seem like anything was different. Edward said, "Listen. Do you hear that faint buzzing? That's how you know it's working." And our reflection on the mirrorlike door disappeared. He said it's creating a bubble of invisibility that we're inside.

"So where do we go from here?" I asked.

"Down. It's an elevator," said Edward. A second or two later, the room plunged downward, fast, so fast almost freefalling. The walls of the room became transparent like a window. The faster we fell, the clearer we could see, as if speed was directly affecting visibility.

As we fell, the enormous cavern got even bigger and brighter. I could see strange spire-shaped buildings soaring upward to incredible heights and ships floating, saucer-shaped ships floating, moving to and fro! "This place was enormous! It's a city!" I exclaimed.

As the elevator stopped at the bottom, I felt no sensation of our ascent being halted! The door opened, and Edward and I stepped out together. "Whoa! We're back outside," I said!

"No! We're in an enormous chamber," said Edward.

"Can't be!" I said. I was seeing blue skies and white clouds with the sun and grass and trees. A creek was near us. I could see a lake in the distance. "What is this place?" I asked.

"I don't know," said Edward, "but there's lots of them in our planet."

This place was enormous! I felt as if I was outside in the middle of nowhere. It didn't feel as though we were deep in the earth. I felt as if I was out in the wilderness!

As Edward and I started to explore, he lowered the mirror shield.

Just then, it started to rain, and a rainbow instantly appeared and so did Hermes! I turned to my left, and there he was standing a few feet away. I started to turn to approach him when I was stopped in my tracks and froze once again. I couldn't move!

He informed Edward and I that we needed to leave this place posthaste! Our interaction with Hermes was much shorter this time. As I stood frozen staring at him, he raised his hand to his chest and was gone! Clearly, he possessed the same type of device we just obtained.

CHAPTER 12

Edward and I wasted no time retreating back to the elevators and into the corridors. Upon exiting the elevator into the corridors, Edward and I were both struck with the memory of Hermes telling us of an event happening today!

Once again, I don't remember Hermes communicating this when we were in the underground place. But I could now recalled the memory as clear as day.

To witness this, Hermes said I would see why human beings are valued as extremely important! Hermes went on to say that throughout all their travels, and all they have come to know only here and with us does a unique and exclusive phenomenon exists.

I was intrigued to say the least. Edward had mentioned their interest of something inside all of us. And now, I might have the chance to actually see what it is they're after!

Edward and I wasted no time making our way through the corridors. It wasn't long before we could see our corridor open up into an already existing corridor.

As we crept slowly along the corridor, Edward and I started to see shadows moving up ahead. Edward motioned for me to stop and stand next to him. Then Edward activated the mirror shield.

We moved slowly forward walking side by side. Quietly, we crept along the wall of the corridor toward the shadows and commotion until we were standing just outside a massive chamber.

We were about to inter the chamber when an alien crossed our path just a few feet in front of us. It looked right at me! I thought, *No way. This won't work. They're going to see us!* Edward could tell I was terrified! "We can't go in. They'll know we're here," I whispered to Edward!

It just seemed that we were out in the open. I didn't feel like I was hiding behind anything. It was hard to tell the mirror shield was working.

Edward said, "Look, one passed right in front of us and didn't see us. As long as we keep our distance, they can't see or hear us." Edward whispered, "They won't find us, unless there looking for us, and they shouldn't be!"

As we rounded the corner into the chamber, there were several aliens busily moving about. I could hear faint unrecognizable dialogue. They were intermingling with one another, waving their hands back and forth and flicking their fingers.

As we made our way farther into the chamber, we moved behind several aliens. I could see their hand gestures and finger movements were in fact controlling visual screens that were seemingly floating in midair in front of them. You could only see this at certain angles!

On a few of the screens, I could see blurs of people's faces. Hundreds, if not thousands, of images within seconds shuffled through as if they were searching.

Several of the other screens made no sense to me. They showed intersecting lines and different-shaped colors and what appeared to be numbers or letters. Some images of people were being rewound and played forward again and again.

In the middle of the chamber, I could see several alcoves, The alcoves were open on both ends. We moved closer, close enough to get a better look, but hopefully not close enough to be detected!

CHAPTER 13

There were four men and three women that I could see. All completely naked. They appeared to be sleeping and floating in various positions. Aliens moved about them, four aliens to each person.

One of the men toward the end of the row near us started to gather attention from the other aliens. He was a middle-aged man with dark hair. Multiple screens started to appear all around this person.

The aliens made gestures with their hands above and around his body, and visual screens appeared from nowhere and displayed functions that apparently are important to the aliens.

At this point, I could see this man's eyes. They were opened and filled with terror! I asked Edward, "What are they doing to him?"

He said, "Filling him with death dreams! Over and over from life to death again and again!"

Before long, there must've been a dozen aliens all buzzing about this one person. Suddenly, a corridor opened on the opposite side of the room from us. A group of four aliens carrying, or floating, what looked to be an older alien in a clear tube.

As they got to the human in distress, the clear tube disappeared, and the old chalk-grayish alien came to float and rest beside the man. Then all but two aliens moved out of the bay, and a glasslike sphere encompassed all four of them.

With hand gestures from the two aliens controlling this procedure, two more spheres appear within the sphere they are in, one around the human man and one around the old alien.

The rest of the aliens in the room gather in front of the bay to watch the spectacle. Edward whispered sternly, "Don't say a word!" There were four to five intensely bright flashes of light.

As the two aliens in the sphere swept their hands across floating screens, you could see something being placed into the man's mind and then his body! He would rise up and arch his back and scream in terror!

It was a visual and emotional wave passing through his body. You could see it! The whole sphere that surrounded him filled with images sweeping through his body again and again.

I watched as the man screamed just before he was beheaded by guillotine and then I was seeing his limbs being torn from his body by horses. I saw and felt the man fall from a great height to his death! Yes, I could feel these emotions as they radiate from the chamber. The next emotion could only be understood as suicide!

With only enough rest for him to catch his breath between sweeping images, I watched as the man experienced being shot in the head, cut down by a sword, eaten alive by dogs, bludgeoned to death with all manner of clubs and hammers, and exploded to bits by bomb! I became saturated by the emotional residue being echoed from the chamber!

Each scene had its own horrific plight that I could feel from a distance. I could feel each image bringing the man closer and closer to the brink of defeat!

The aliens did this over and over, and a bridge of gold light started to appear between the man and the old alien. As the man screamed for what would be the last time, I could see a ball, an orb of silverish-blue-white light about the size of a baseball, rise up from the man's chest and began to traverse across the bridge of golden light toward the alien.

As it reached the center of this golden light bridge, the silverish-blue-white light pulsed once and then started drawing back into the man. Then the orb stopped and started to be drawn in by the alien.

With the orb being drawn in by the man and the alien, it appeared to be some type of tug-of-war taking place.

With the man now dead, the old alien still alive gave what could only be described as a sinister grin as the majority of the orb increasingly drew to his favor!

As I watched the last of the orb being absorbed into the old alien, the light bridge collapsed and disappeared in a flash. The alien took its last breath and was dead! Then it was over, with the excitement over the aliens started to disperse.

Edward and I were able to get a little closer to see what remained in the bay. We could see both the man and the alien floating lifelessly. They were clearly dead!

CHAPTER 14

Edward said, "Okay, we been here long enough. Let's make our way back."

I said, "What about the other people? Is there anything we can do to help them?"

"Not here, not now! Don't talk! We got to get back!" said Edward. "Take the lead. You know how to get us back."

I said, "I do?"

He said, "Yeah, you have points of references now. Do you remember where we started?"

"Yeah, yeah. I remember," I said.

Edward lowered the mirror shield after we got a ways away from the chamber. He said, "Just keep walking and thinking about where you want to go, and the tunnel will do the rest." Edward knew I had a lot of questions. He said, "Let's keep going. We'll talk when we get out of here."

As we walked through the smooth tunnel, I started feeling that sensation of movement again. I started thinking how fast we must be moving through the earth. I felt hazy and a little dizzy. I found myself navigating through the tunnels fairly easy. It wasn't long before we reached our hazmat suits.

As we made our way through the false water, out of the tunnels, and back to the car, Edward could tell I wanted answers. We started driving, and Edward started talking. He told me the story Hermes told him. He said, "The aliens that are here now have been here since the beginning of our creation!"

Edward told me about a race of beings that came to be in the universe. As they grew, so did their technology, becoming star travelers. They visited countless planets throughout the universe. Becoming so advanced, they came to understand their own purpose.

Existing for millennia, their belief adopted through time and technology. They've come to know that there is indeed a creator god. And their purpose is to hasten life, and they proudly fulfill their purpose—existing to influence and manipulation to the fullest potential the life they encountered.

When they came to our planet thousands and thousands of years ago, they influenced our form of life and intentionally sped up the inevitable evolution we were destined for.

But upon observing our evolution, they noticed something different. Different from anything else they had ever encountered. They noticed upon our death, something briefly remained. Of all the other life they've encountered and had a hand in accelerating, we were different!

They experimented and studied our deaths for thousands of years to finally understand what's happening. They found that within our birth, we are given a vessel, a vessel in which our essence along with our emotions and understanding of this reality can travel back to the place we were before our birth!

"You're talking about are souls aren't you?" I asked Edward.

"Yep, that's what we call it," Edward said. He went on to tell me why they are taking people. For a long time now, they've had the ability to remove our essence and fill the vessel with theirs, effectively replacing us!

CHAPTER 15

Edward explained, "You see, their majority decided since they increase the speed of our evolution, essentially creating us. They were more entitled to continue than we were. Their race is divided. The ones that disagree, stand against them. Within their belief, the creator god has a purpose for them. They will not be takers! So they help us when they can, and they have been doing so for thousands of years. It's not easy for them to do since our entire world has been sculpted by the takers." Edward said, "It's like I said. People got it all wrong! Most of the people that believe aliens are here believe they're here for the wrong reasons."

"You're telling me they're here for our souls?" I asked Edward. "And they're killing us to take it! Game over!" I said.

"There's nothing we can do! They can't just kill us," said Edward.

"What do you mean?" I asked.

Edward told me more about how reincarnations is real. He said, "Killing us just sends us back where we started, and we come back again, being born, that is. They can only take from a life that is destined for death in the true timeline."

When monitoring a human, and they find that their death is upon them, they will stop time moments before their death, back time up, and place them in their lab. If all conditions are right, and the alien assigned to take the human soul is near death but strong, they can seize eternity for themselves!

Hermes told Edward that their observations found our purpose is to return to this reality and live a life as many times as we can until, well, until whatever this is has completed. Edward said, "Hermes believes we are filling an expanse with experiences from reality. And when it's full, this universe will end! And all those that have made it over, so to speak, will continue on to what comes next!"

Edward said Hermes explained it to him like this, "You are a bee that left the beehive. You land on a flower, and your life begins. You gather up pollen, and you are living. You return to the hive, and you are dead, bringing what you had gathered while you were alive!"

Edward exclaimed, "No! They won't just kill us, but they do keep tabs on all of us. It's like a global network around the planet, and we are their crops. They observe us to see when we are right for harvest!"

"And what makes us right for harvest?" I asked.

CHAPTER 16

"The easiest ones for them to take are those that never questioned life!" Edward said, "Those that wonder often of what happens after death and picture places to be and believe in the possibility of existing after they're dead, the continued thoughts of this nature touches their soul in a way that binds them stronger to it! For those, it is not impossible, but it is harder for the aliens to pry free their prize!"

The drive to my house seem quick. As I got out of the car, Edward said, "I know it's a lot to take in! Get some sleep. I'll be back in a couple days."

I barely remember walking into my house. I remember eating everything in sight, taking a shower, and falling asleep. I felt out of sync with reality! I was waking up and falling asleep over and over again! One minute dreaming, the next minute awake and remembering!!

Two days later, Edward was at my door with another excursion. We drove a short distance out of town and arrived at an abandoned farmhouse. The old farmhouse was mostly in shambles, the kind of place most people wouldn't even go into.

Splintered wood, broken boards, and barely a roof. It looked like the whole place could collapse at any time! We stepped up on the creaking porch, opened the half-broken door, and walked into the place. There were a couple of sticks of old furniture and a broom.

I asked Edward, "Where do we go?"

Edward said, "The back door."

We walked over to the back door, and Edward pushed it open. For a second, I thought I was dreaming! Once again, I was caught off guard frozen in my tracks. For just outside the door stood Hermes.

Seeing Hermes was shocking enough, but I was blown away by where we now were. We were in an underground alien base that housed dozens of different types of craft.

I was about to ask Edward if these were all spaceships. But before I started to speak, Hermes communicated to me that these were the same type of craft I've been seeing in the night sky. Fortunately for us, the place was empty except for Hermes.

Hermes communicated to us that he wished to take us on a short trip. I was hearing his communication, but I could not move a muscle. He explained to us that we would be able to move freely as long as we follow his will.

Hermes turned from us and started walking toward a ship, a classic UFO-shape ship. Suddenly, I was able to move. I looked at Edward, and we started to follow Hermes. As we neared the ship, I noticed a curious object to my right.

When I started to observe the object more intently to try to understand what it was, I found myself growing sluggish and stiffening. As I looked back toward Hermes and resumed following, I once again became free with motion. I knew then instantly what Hermes meant when he said follow his will.

We boarded the ship. Inside looked milky gray white and smooth like the corridors, and there was no place to sit. In an instant, we were flying out of a canyon. The scenery went by like a blur. I felt no movement or motion. Then the planet was behind us, and we were in space! And I could see the moon getting bigger and bigger and bigger!

CHAPTER 17

It seemed we were going to crash into the moon. An instant later, we were disembarking the ship that had safely landed. Hermes had us follow him to an observation area. Hermes waved his hand, and a cloudy dome in front and above us became crystal clear, and I could see the Earth magnified.

As I watched the screen, different-colored filters started to appear and overlay the screen or dome or whatever this thing was I was looking through. And I could see silvery streaks, tracers from objects, tiny objects going to and from the Earth.

I didn't know what I was looking at. There were thousands of tiny silvery things streaking toward and away from Earth! Another filter went up on the screen. Suddenly half the streaks were tented in a reddish-green color, and the other half remain silvery.

As I wondered, Hermes explained it plain as day! Hermes said, "Half of your species' destiny is now ours! And every day, it increases slightly more in our favor."

Hermes said it has taken time, but now, most all of his kind are coming. And all of them will be here by the time the population on the planet doubles.

This conveyance of information by Hermes felt different. There was an overwhelming sense of urgency, despair, doom, and regret! With my senses overwhelmed, I felt numb!

Edward said, "Now you know!"

"I know. I know," I said. "I know I'm not supposed to know this! I know that! What would they do to us for knowing this?" I asked.

"I don't know, but I know it wouldn't be good," said Edward.

Hermes started telling us how we could get back to Earth by ourselves when suddenly, the screen went blank. Hermes's conveyance became rapid. We had been discovered, and the others were on their way!

Hermes told Edward and I where we could find escape pods. It was strange. In an instance, I was given all the information I needed by Hermes to operate the pod. I knew that the pods were like spaceships, but they would only last one trip. I knew that the pods can travel from the moon to the Earth and that was it. And after landing, the pods would disintegrate!

Hermes released us from his will. And Edward and I began running toward the escape pods. I glanced back, and Hermes was gone. Edward and I were on our own! It wasn't long before we reached the pods.

CHAPTER 18

In a narrow hallway, there were two pods opposite each other. Alien tech was required, so Edward grabbed the mirror shield device, placed it on his fingers, and waved his hand in front of the wall, and the pod opened. Edward then handed me the mirror shield device so I could do the same to my escape pod.

We entered our pods, and as the escape pods were closing and readying for launch, I saw a gray alien coming down the hallway heading our way. I thought for a moment it was Hermes coming to help. It was not!

The only thing I could think to do was activate the mirror shield while I was in the escape pod. I didn't know if it would work or not, but I did it anyway. I rose my hand to my chest and rendered myself invisible!

I watched as the alien glanced my way, then turn toward Edward. Our launches had been aborted. I could sense the conveyance by this alien toward Edward. I couldn't sense anger from the alien, just terrible intentions!

Helpless and in silence, I watched as the aliens set upon Edward's pod a time disk and resume his pod's launch sequence. As the pod was beginning to launch, the alien did something to hold it in place and sent time spinning.

I watched as the pod sped through time until it reached its point of disintegration. With Edward still inside, the pod was rapidly stripped away molecule by molecule, atom by atom. Edward said nothing as his molecules started separating. The pod and Edward soon became a swirling blur. Within a few seconds, nothing remained, not even Edward!

I can't believe I just watched Edward die! Now I was alone in this place! With Edward gone, I wasn't sure what to do. I just needed to get back to Earth!

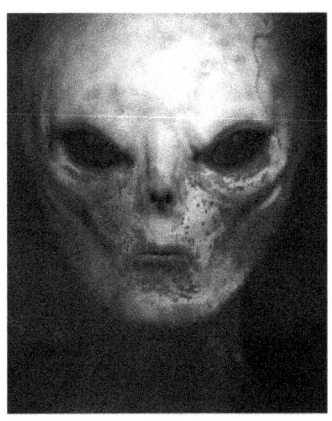

CHAPTER 19

I hid behind the mirror shield, just hoping not to be discovered. The mirror shield started to fail, and I could see an alien clearing a hole like wiping steam from a mirror and peering in. He found me!

I could only think to cover my face with my hands like a child in hopes he wouldn't see me. Peering through my fingers like a frightened child, I watched as the alien set the time disk upon my pod. I can only imagine my fate was to be the same as Edward!

Darkness, I could see. I don't know what I'm looking at. Trying to focus, I don't know what I'm seeing. Dreadful feelings turning me inside out and leaving me hollow!

Feeling despair and hopelessness, repeating, endless repeating! Unable to grasp time, unsure of when now is!

Hungry, sickly hot, and cold. Skull pounding head, never-ending pain. Unceasing. How long? How long is this? Every ounce of my resistance cannot find relief from this place!

Spinning now. Spinning faster and faster. Yes, definitely spinning. This is different. This must be now! Spinning so fast now, too fast. The pain! Much, much too fast! I feel as if I am tearing! I don't think it's going to stop!

Just then, an abrupt stop! It felt like hitting a wall, and I found myself on the floor of an empty room.

As I lay on the floor of this empty room battered and beaten, he stepped out from behind a mirror shield. It's Hermes. He found me! Hermes informed me that forty-five Earth years had gone by. Hermes said, "The one that has detained me will not be pleased if he finds you have escaped."

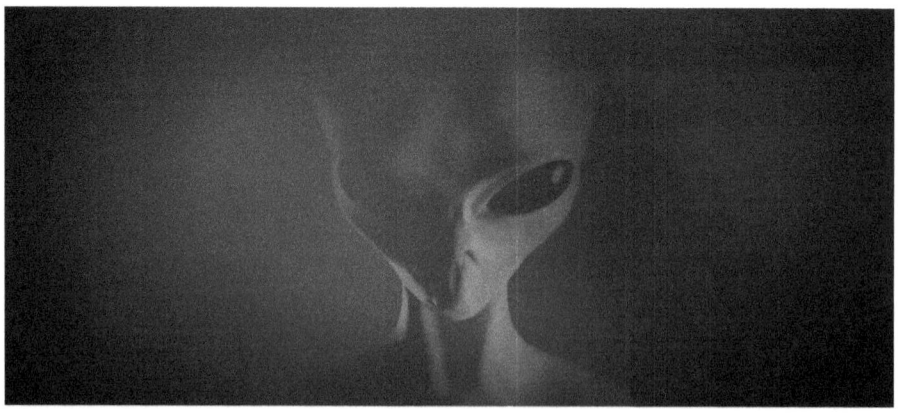

Hermes said the only way to free me was to send me back in time. He told me this time, I needed to inform others along with my earlier self about what was happening. "This time," I mumbled. I wanted to question his information. But once again, he wasn't exactly talking directly to me.

He made it clear I could not reveal my true identity. He stressed there would be grave consequences if I did! I told Hermes I was worried I'd be recognized. Hermes remind me that forty-five years of my life had gone by, and I had endured much torture in that time, and I did not resemble the person I once was.

As he led me to a time travel device and set it upon me, a bubble formed around me and started to shimmer.

CHAPTER 20

As I started colliding through time, things around me started to blur faster and faster. Then an abrupt stop! I felt my brain bounce off my skull! I was wondering, *Did I arrive?* Before I had time to think another thought, two alien hands reached in to my time bubble and seize my will!

As things slowly started to come into focus, I could see it was the one who detained me. While the time bubble was halted from spinning, his message to me was brief and simple: he could not stop the timeline set in motion.

But he had every intention to interfere. "See if you can hide when you go back like you tried to hide from me!" he conveyed.

In an instant without my doing, my hands were thrust onto my face. The time bubble started swirling again. The alien's hands withdrew, and the last thing I heard in my head, "Was let it burn!"

The message from him echoing again and again, "Let it burn!" All of my efforts to move were met with the inability to know how. I couldn't feel how to tell myself to move. I was paralyzed.

As this sickening, dizzying feeling from the spinning time bubble lessened, the bubble started to disappear. I found myself sitting in the middle of a dark and dank dirty alleyway with my hands cupped to my face.

As I regain some feeling and started to move, my thoughts for motion to move my hands are met with failure. I try to free them from my face, and I can't. It was as if I lost the ability to control them.

Just then, I heard his message one last time echoing in my head, "Let it burn!" My face and skull started to sear. I could feel burning at my fingertips reaching deep into my brain!

I had to make it stop. I got to my feet and started running the best I could. My legs weren't working well. My eyes were watering. I couldn't see. The pain was excruciating! I thought my head was going to explode!

As I stumbled out of the alleyway, strength started returning to my hands. I was yelling and flailing about. I just wanted the burning to stop. The more strength that returned to my hands, the harder I tugged. Such intense burning!

Frantic and panicking! Harder and harder, I try to get my hands free from my face as I yank, rip, and tear. Finally, one hand comes free, and the burning stops!

Just ahead, I hear a voice. It sounds familiar! It's me. I'm standing by my car! O my god. I'm Edward!

The end.

ABOUT THE AUTHOR

Kenneth W. Polack, it seems, was destined to ponder the mysterious. On the day of his birth, September 8, 1966, A sci-fi phenomenon was exploding across the country. In fact, his birth coincides with the debut of the show and sci-fi sensation *Star Trek*! The world exploding with science fiction, Kenneth Polack felt he fit right in. But he also felt maybe his time spent imagining fanciful things was something an intelligent person would not spend so much time doing. Then a quote came his way: "The most beautiful thing we can experience is the mysterious, but he to whom that emotion is a stranger and cannot pause to ponder, they are as good dead. Their eyes are shut!" From someone who the whole world would say possessed intelligence, Albert Einstein. Learning this widened Kenneth Polack's scope. His imagination unbound. He explores and pokes at the mysteries hidden in our reality of smoke.

www.ingramcontent.com/pod-product-compliance
Lightning Source LLC
Chambersburg PA
CBHW051237120626
46547CB00013B/1677